Hi!

This book belongs to:

____

I Can, You Can, We can pray!

By

Keith Ponto

On a beautiful morning, Miss Ellie happily said,
"Welcome to kids' church, everyone!"
The children beamed at her, but soon a sob
broke out from the joyful crowd.
Every head turned to Jack, a little
boy who was always the happiest
one of them all. Sadly, though,
Jack sat in the back corner,
crying alone.

"Jack, what's wrong?" Miss Ellie asked.
Jack answered with a sob and a sniffle, "My mom is in the hospital, and she is not well."
Miss Ellie's eyes shone with compassion as she laid a gentle hand on Jack's shoulder. "You know, Jack, the Heavenly Father can heal your mom."

Jack looked up, his eyes bright with tears. "Can He make her better, so she can come home to us again?" Miss Ellie smiled and nodded confidently. "Yes, God can make your mom well."

Then, turning to face the other children, Miss Ellie said, "Come, children, let's pray for Jack's mom. Let's ask God to heal her so that she can go home to be with her family."

The children moved to the rug in the
center of the room and sat down in a
circle as Miss Ellie and Jack joined them.
"Can anyone pray? Sam asked.
"Yes, anyone can pray. I can.
You and you and you can pray. We all
can pray!" replied Miss Ellie,
smiling at every child.
"I didn't know that,"
Sam said in wonder.
"How does a person
pray?" Peter asked.

"It's like talking to your mom and dad," Miss Ellie
said. "Would you like me to teach you how to pray?"
"Yes!" the children shouted.

Miss Ellie smiled proudly at them and nodded. "Do
you know you can pray anytime? But the best time
would be when you get up in the morning and when
you go to bed in the evening."
The children shook their heads, staring at her with
curiosity.

"Prayer seems difficult," Peter commented.
"Not at all," Miss Ellie said.
"In the Bible, we read in Matthew 6:9-13.

Jesus taught His disciples to pray."
She said, "First, you need to say,
Our Father in heaven."
"Miss Ellie, is God my father?"
Sarah asked.

"Yes, Sarah! God is our Father, and Jesus wanted us to
know that. God is our Father in heaven," Miss Ellie
explained.
"Wow, I have two fathers!" Jane exclaimed with a big
smile on her face. I have my dad and my Heavenly Father!
"Let me continue," Miss Ellie said. "God is our Father in
Heaven. We are all God's children. That is why the Lord's
prayer starts like this,

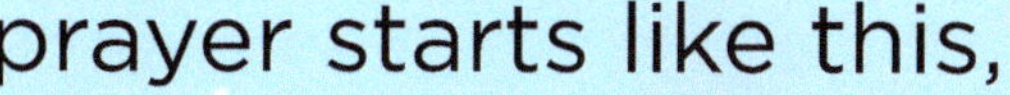

Our Father in Heaven, hallowed be your name," Miss Ellie
explains. "We need to be thankful and grateful to God for
everything He has done for us."

Then, her eyes met Lucy's, who was eagerly
bouncing. Miss Ellie asked her, "Do you know
what being thankful and grateful is?"
Lucy thought about it but eventually shook
her head.
"To be thankful is to say thank you when you
are given a gift, and to be grateful is when
you have a lot of toys when your friends
don't have toys or food. We are also thankful
and grateful for our health and our family,"
Miss Ellie explained.

"I'm thankful!" Lucy said.
"That's wonderful, Lucy.
All of us must be grateful.

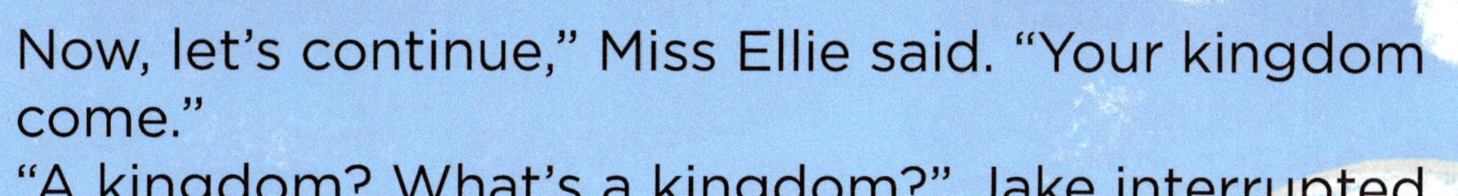

Now, let's continue," Miss Ellie said. "Your kingdom come."

"A kingdom? What's a kingdom?" Jake interrupted. "You know we have a queen here in England, right? England is a kingdom, and the Queen rules over it. And God, like the Queen, rules over His Kingdom," Miss Ellie explained as best she could, then continued with the Lord's prayer.

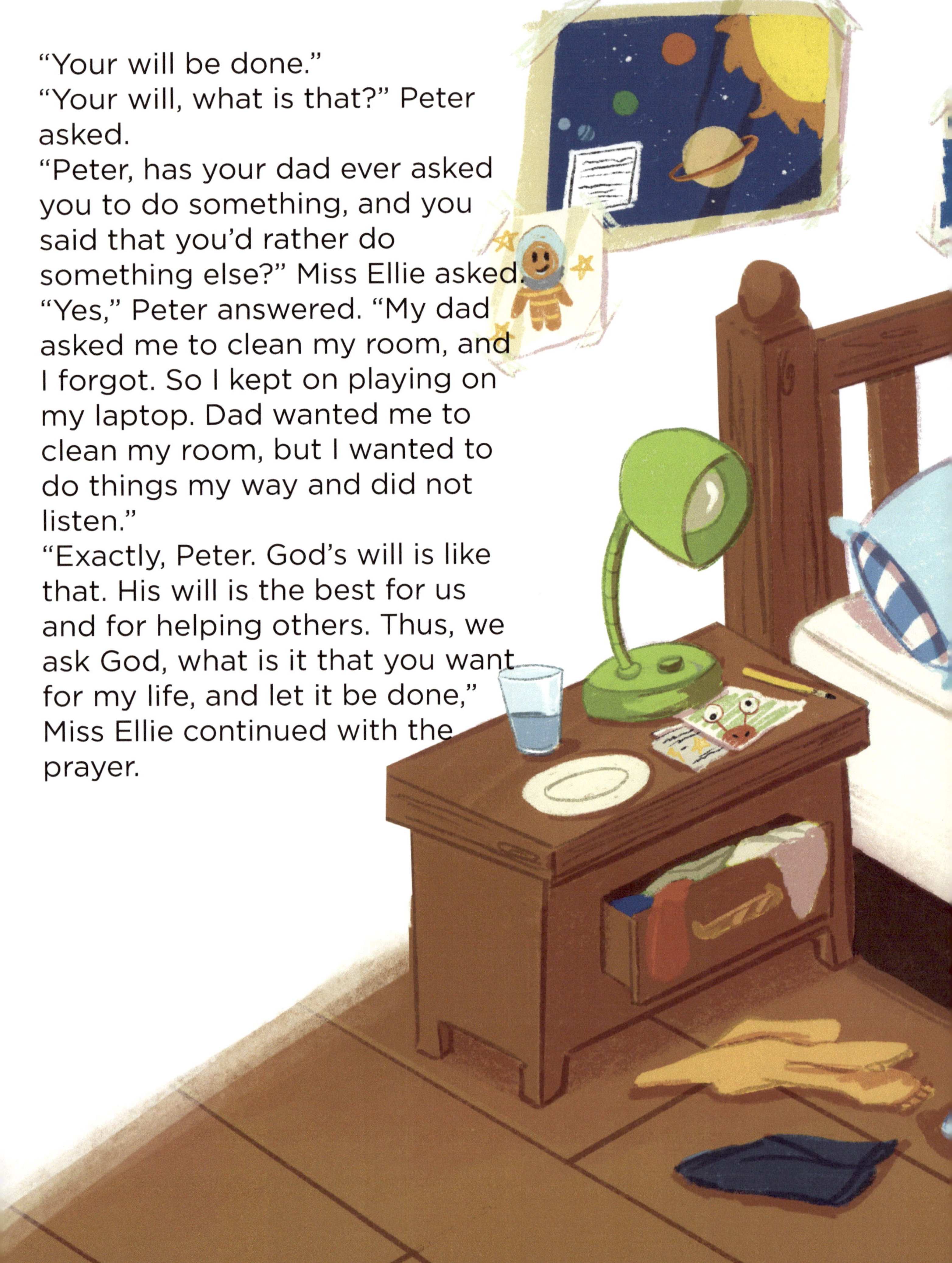

"Your will be done."

"Your will, what is that?" Peter asked.

"Peter, has your dad ever asked you to do something, and you said that you'd rather do something else?" Miss Ellie asked.

"Yes," Peter answered. "My dad asked me to clean my room, and I forgot. So I kept on playing on my laptop. Dad wanted me to clean my room, but I wanted to do things my way and did not listen."

"Exactly, Peter. God's will is like that. His will is the best for us and for helping others. Thus, we ask God, what is it that you want for my life, and let it be done," Miss Ellie continued with the prayer.

"On earth as it is in heaven."
"Miss Ellie, Miss Ellie?" Sam asked. "I don't understand what you are saying about on earth as in heaven."
"Are you in heaven, Sam?" Miss Ellie asked.
"Oh no, I'm still alive, and I'm here on Earth!" Sam said with a giggle.
Jake laughed. "No, Miss Ellie, we are still here on Earth. In heaven, there is no crying, no pain, or suffering."

"There is a lot of joy and peace. There's no fighting or shouting, like here on Earth," added Peter.
"There's no hunger and no hurting," added Miss Ellie. "We want for everything to be as good and beautiful here on Earth, as it is in heaven."

Miss Ellie continued with the prayer, "Give us today our daily bread."

"I don't like bread," Jane protested.

"My mother always gives me bread."

"I like it when my mom makes me chicken sandwiches," said Sarah, giggling.

"Jane, there are children that don't have bread as we do, so we can ask God to give them bread and everything that they need. We can ask God for everything we need," Miss Ellie explained.

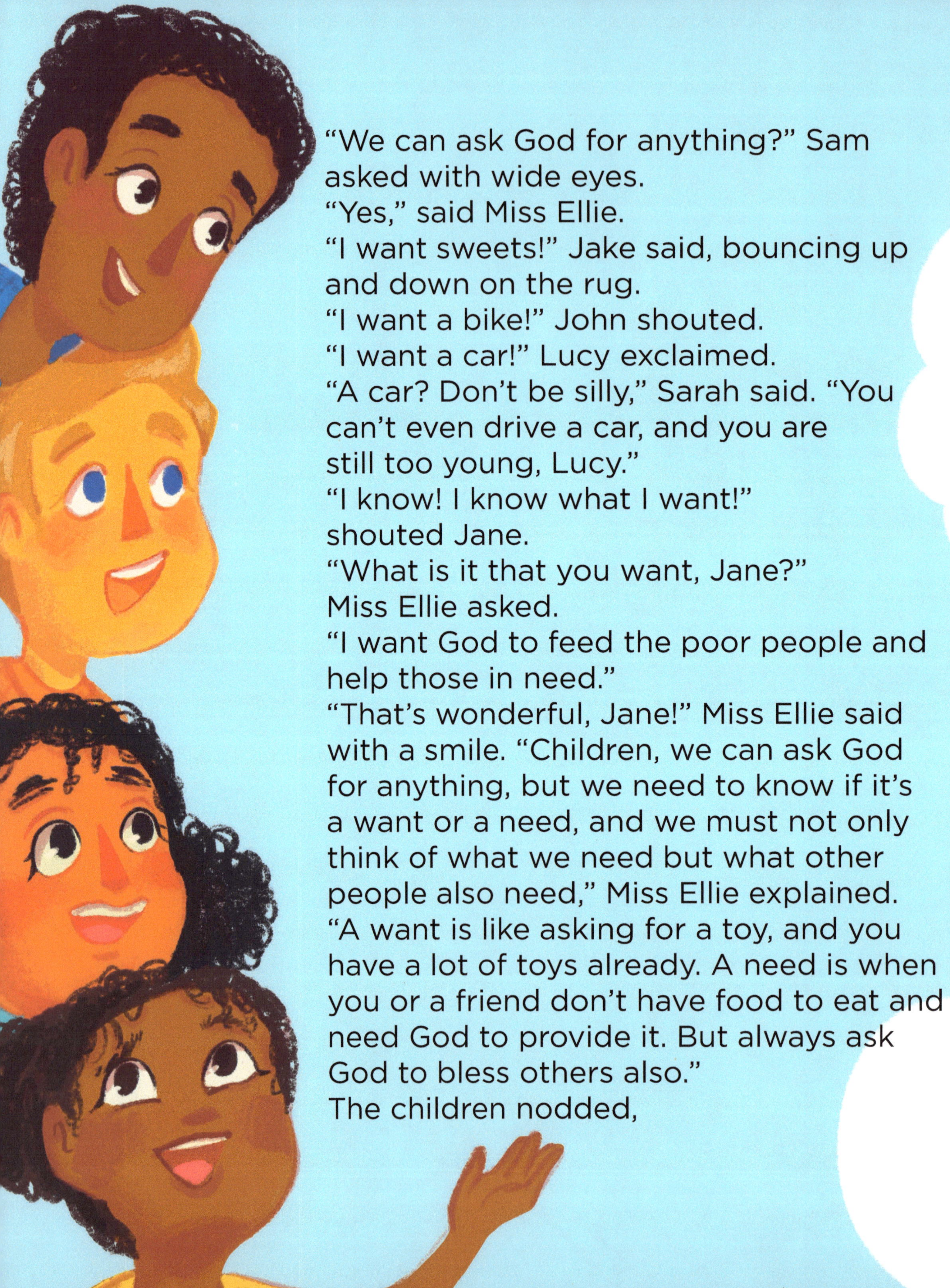

"We can ask God for anything?" Sam
asked with wide eyes.
"Yes," said Miss Ellie.
"I want sweets!" Jake said, bouncing up
and down on the rug.
"I want a bike!" John shouted.
"I want a car!" Lucy exclaimed.
"A car? Don't be silly," Sarah said. "You
can't even drive a car, and you are
still too young, Lucy."
"I know! I know what I want!"
shouted Jane.
"What is it that you want, Jane?"
Miss Ellie asked.
"I want God to feed the poor people and
help those in need."
"That's wonderful, Jane!" Miss Ellie said
with a smile. "Children, we can ask God
for anything, but we need to know if it's
a want or a need, and we must not only
think of what we need but what other
people also need," Miss Ellie explained.
"A want is like asking for a toy, and you
have a lot of toys already. A need is when
you or a friend don't have food to eat and
need God to provide it. But always ask
God to bless others also."
The children nodded,

Miss Ellie continued to say the next part of the prayer,
"And forgive us our debts. We need to ask God to
forgive our debts."
"What are debts?" asked John.
"Debt, John, is when you asked someone to let
you borrow money, and you need to pay it back.
Likewise, when you do something wrong like taking
something without permission, then you need to ask for
forgiveness."

"Like stealing?" said Jane.
"Yes," said Miss Ellie.
"I know!" Peter said.
"What do you know, Peter?" Miss Ellie asked.
"It's like telling a white lie."
"Yes, Peter," said Miss Ellie. "Children, don't ever say a
white lie or a small lie. A lie is a lie, and we always need to
be honest."
The children nodded, and Miss Ellie continued,

"As we also have forgiven our debtors."
"I know what debtors mean," shouted Lucy, raising her hand.
"What does it mean, Lucy?" Miss Ellie asked.
"It means, it means, it means." Lucy struggled to find words.
"What, Lucy?" Sam asked.
Lucy shrugged and looked down.
Miss Ellie smiled. "It means owing someone some-thing. It's almost the same as debts, but debtors are those who owe us something and never pay us back. This is sometimes hard to do, but we need to learn to forgive someone if they did us wrong."
The children nodded, and Miss Ellie went on to say, "And lead us not into temptation. Have you ever seen something that you liked, and no one is around to see what you were doing?"
The children nodded quickly.
"If you took something that's not yours, it is stealing!" Jake shouted. "It is stealing, and it's wrong!"

"Yes, it's wrong," said Miss Ellie, "but what do you do if you see a toy that is not yours? How do you bring yourself to leave it and not take it? How do you walk away?"

"That's so difficult," complained Peter.

John raised his hand. "Miss Ellie, so temptation is to walk away from something wrong?"

"Yes, John," said Miss Ellie.

When the children grew quiet once more, Miss
Ellie continued to say, "But deliver us from the
evil one. Deliver us from the one that wants bad
things to happen to us. God is protecting us."

"I don't want bad things to happen to us." Lucy
whimpered.
"God will always protect us and keep us from
harm and danger. God loves us very much, and He
always wants us to talk to Him and tell Him how
we feel," Miss Ellie said reassuringly.

"Let's say the Lord's Prayer
together now."
"Our Father in heaven,
hallowed be your name,
your kingdom come,
your will be done, on earth
as it is in heaven.
Give us today our daily bread.
And forgive us our debts,
as we also have forgiven
our debtors.
And lead us not into temptation,
but deliver us from the evil.
For thine is the kingdom,
and the power, And the glory,
forever and ever.
Amen."

The children echoed her words and looked up with bright smiles.
"Remember, before you go to sleep and when you get up in the morning, talk to God and know that He loves us very much," Miss Ellie said to the children as the bells for the end of morning service chimed.

As parents began to pick their children up, a familiar person entered the classroom.

"Good morning, Miss Ellie," greeted Jack's dad. "I just want to share the good news with Jack that we must go and get his mom from the hospital."

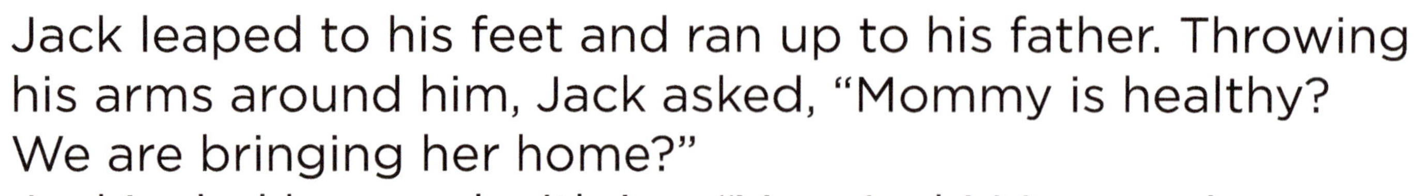

Jack leaped to his feet and ran up to his father. Throwing his arms around him, Jack asked, "Mommy is healthy? We are bringing her home?"
Jack's dad beamed with joy. "Yes, Jack! Mommy is healthy, and the doctor said she can come home with us today."
"That's certainly excellent news," said Miss Ellie.
Jack's dad wrapped him in an embrace.

"We prayed for her today," Miss Ellie remarked.
"Is that so?" Jack's dad asked.
Jack happily nodded as he grabbed his dad's hand, and the two walked towards the door, "God heard our prayer, Dad."
"He did, and now Mommy is all better!" Dad agreed.

"Remember to Pray for someone today and don't forget to pray for yourself"

I Can, You Can, We can pray!

For Preteens

Coming Soon!!!!

For more information contact:
pontopublishing@gmail.com

Bye!

www.ingramcontent.com/pod-product-compliance
Lightning Source LLC
Chambersburg PA
CBHW042124030726
47599CB00002B/339